ERIC CLAPTON

ERIC CLAPTON

FRED WEILER

BISON GROUP

First published in 1992 by
Bison Books Ltd
Kimbolton House
117A Fulham Road
London SW3 6RL

ISBN 0-86124-941-0

Printed in Hong Kong

Below: Eric Clapton (left) with Jack Bruce (center) and Ginger Baker (right) in Cream, the British supergroup that catapulted Clapton from blues purism to rock stardom.

ACKNOWLEDGMENTS

Three works were of critical use to me in writing this book: John Pidgeon's *Eric Clapton*, Ray Coleman's *Clapton!* (originally entitled *Survivor!* in the U.K.), and Harry Shapiro's *Slowhand: The Story of Eric Clapton*. Whenever referring to them in this book, I have used just the author names. Marc Roberty's *Eric Clapton: A Visual Documentary* was also a valuable resource.

Thanks to John Efron and my editor, Jean Martin, for helping to shape the manuscript into a polished production. But most of all, I would like to thank my wife, Beth, for her unflagging support – and for enduring more Eric Clapton music than any mortal should have to hear in one lifetime.

Thanks also go to the designer, Don Longabucco; the photo researcher, Sara Dunphy; and the indexer, Elizabeth A. McCarthy.

PICTURE CREDITS

Brompton Photo Library: pages 9(bottom), 14(bottom right), 24, 55, 65, 68.
Alec Byrne/Relay Photos: page 33.
Andre Csillag/Relay Photos: pages 80-81.
Alan Davidson/Globe Photos: page 86(top).
Tony De Nonno/Globe Photos: pages 61, 64(bottom right).
Steve Emberton/Relay Photos: pages 72-73
Chris Fallo: pages 19, 36, 44, 50, 75(top), 84.
Tony Gale/Pictorial Press: pages 12, 18.
Dezo Hoffman/Rex Ltd.: page 34.
Jorgensen/Rex Ltd.: page 85(top).
Robert Minkin: pages 37, 88, 89(top).
Stephen Morely/David Redfern Photography: page 78.
Ilpo Musto/Rex Ltd.: page 1.
Dave Parker/Globe Photos: page 85(bottom right).
Ed Perlstein/Globe Photos: page 79.
Photofest: pages 7, 16-17, 40(bottom), 41, 76-77, 85(bottom left).
Pictorial Press: pages 10-11, 21, 22-23, 25(both), 26-27, 28-29, 31, 32, 35(both), 38-39, 42, 43, 62-63, 66, 67, 70.
D. Rankin/Globe Photos: page 89(bottom).
Relay Photos: pages 4-5, 6, 45, 60, 82.
Rex Ltd.: pages 71, 86(bottom), 87.
Ken Settle/Relay Photos: page 2.
Joseph Sia: pages 49, 51(top), 52-53, 69.
UPI/Bettmann Newsphotos: pages 9(top), 13, 15, 20, 51(bottom), 56, 57, 75(bottom).
Chris Walter/Relay Photos: pages 46-47, 58-59, 74, 81(right).
Fred Weiler Collection: pages 8, 14(top), 14(bottom left), 30, 40(top), 48, 54, 64(bottom left), 91.

Contents

Introduction

For more than 25 years, rock audiences have been acclaiming Eric Clapton as the world's greatest rock guitarist – and for just as long, Clapton has been trying to live down that reputation. Bursting forth on the British music scene in the early 1960s with a fiery blues style, he inspired graffiti proclaiming that 'Clapton Is God' and played a vital role in shaping the sound of rock guitar. Today, Eric Clapton is mentioned in the same breath as such guitar heroes as Jimi Hendrix, Jeff Beck, and Jimmy Page.

The photos on the back cover of the *History of Eric Clapton* album show Clapton's uncanny ability to change his physical appearance within a short span of time. Similarly, Eric the musician is constantly reinventing himself, zigzagging from the imitative R&B of the Yardbirds to the electric blues of John Mayall's Bluesbreakers to the free-form jazz-rock of Cream. During the 1960s, he walked out on commercially successful musical projects at unexpected times, confounding the expectations of his fans.

Clapton's solo career has had its ups and downs, as he struggled first with heroin, then with alcohol. During the 1970s, he turned away from guitar pyrotechnics, dabbling in reggae and crafting a subtle, pop-flavored sound. Eric's concerts were wildly uneven as he nervously searched for a musical direction, patterning his music on such low-key artists as J.J. Cale and Don Williams. Longtime fans yearned for the flashy guitar licks of his Cream and Derek & the Dominos period. But starting in the mid-1980s, Clapton pulled out of this slump and garnered a new generation of fans. He sings and plays nowadays with exuberance and self-confidence, recording albums that are far more focused than his 1970s efforts.

At the core of Clapton's music – through all his permutations, from blues purist to unabashed balladeer – are two qualities. The first is the unmatched lyricism of his playing, the emotion that he can wring from his guitar with seemingly little effort. This artistry is what links Eric's dobro solo on 1989's 'Running on Faith,' for example, with his similar work on a song from 1974's *461 Ocean Boulevard*, 'Let It Grow.' The second constant in Eric's career is his passion for the blues, and his reverence for the musical heroes that inspired him. Ever since his superstar days with Cream, Clapton has acknowledged the pioneers who laid the groundwork for his own accomplishments: B.B. King, Freddie King, Buddy Guy, Muddy Waters. As he explained in an MTV documentary: 'I'm very proud of the fact that I helped in some way or another the real bluesmen to get exposure. For me, as I remember it now, the original idea was to actually say, "Hey, I didn't start this, they did" . . . To do that, to have successfully done that, was what it was all about for me.'

Above: Eric Clapton in 1967. In his two-and-a-half years with Cream, he changed hairstyles and fashions with astonishing frequency.

Below: The changing faces of a chameleon-like Clapton, from 1966 to 1970.

Below: Eric today, playing his favorite guitar, 'Blackie.' Second guitarist Phil Palmer is in the background.

Opposite top: Eric with Jeff Healy, Tina Turner, and Keith Richards at the International Rock Awards in New York, 31 May 1989.

Opposite bottom: Clapton dueling with B.B. King on *B.B. King & Friends*, a cable TV special subsequently released on home video.

Steppin' Out—The Yardbirds and John Mayall's Bluesbreakers

Eric Patrick Clapton was born in Ripley, in the south of England, on 30 March 1945, the illegitimate son of Patricia Clapton and a Canadian soldier. Shortly after Eric was born, his mother went to Europe and left him to be raised by her parents, Jack and Rose Clapp. But when Eric turned 12, Patricia Clapton returned to live with the Clapps for a short time, and Eric learned of his illegitimacy.

Previous pages: Keith Relf, Paul Samwell-Smith, Chris Dreja, Eric Clapton, and Jim McCarty – The Yardbirds, 1964.

Below: A 19-year-old Clapton grinning mischievously in London's Hyde Park.

Growing up, he felt different from other boys, and became something of a loner. When he wasn't playing with his snail collection, Eric would spend hours in front of the radio, soaking up the sounds of Muddy Waters, Big Bill Broonzy, Ray Charles, and B.B. King.

The adolescent Clapton was mesmerized by the blues records from America that he heard, and he was not alone – a whole gener-

Left: B.B. King, a major influence on the British blues boom of the early 1960s. During Cream's first visit to America in 1967, Eric had his first opportunity to jam with King.

ation of aspiring British youngsters was drawn to the raw-boned sounds coming over on Chess Records out of Chicago. Since Eric regarded himself as an outsider, the heroic quality of this exotic music strongly appealed to him. 'I felt through most of my youth that my back was against the wall,' Eric explained to Melvyn Bragg on BBC-TV's 'South Bank Show' (1987). 'The only way to survive that was with dignity, pride, and courage, and I heard that . . . most of all in the blues. It was always one man with his guitar versus the world . . . one guy who was completely alone with no options, no alternatives whatsoever, other than to sing and play to ease his pain.'

At age 14 or 15, Clapton got his first guitar, a £14 acoustic that he talked the Clapps into buying him. His fascination with the blues took him to record shops to dig up Little Walter and John Lee Hooker imports. He started with a few simple chords, and before long, he could play Muddy Waters and Chuck Berry licks backwards and forwards.

In 1962, Eric, having shown a natural artistic ability, attended Kingston College of Art and studied stained-glass design. Attending art school was a typical course of action for many of the British youngsters who would later become big names on the rock scene, such as Keith Richards, Pete Townshend,

Top left: Lightnin' Hopkins (1912-82) was a country-blues singer from Texas who played rock venues throughout the 1960s.

Top right: The guitar style of Albert King, a.k.a. the Velvet Bulldozer, shines through Clapton's solo on Cream's 'Strange Brew.'

Bottom right: The ever-flamboyant Little Richard, a key figure in 1950s rock and roll.

Bottom left: When Muddy Waters toured with Eric in 1979, the bluesman would often refer to Clapton as his 'adopted son.'

Opposite: On his *Journeyman* LP, Eric finally paid tribute to Ray Charles – one of his musical heroes – with a version of Ray's 'Hard Times.'

and the Kinks' Ray Davies. Clapton was drawn to some of the musicians shaking up the London club scene – people like Mick Jagger, Brian Jones, Ginger Baker, and Jack Bruce, all of whom played with Alex Korner's Blues Incorporated.

Blues Incorporated was England's first authentic R & B band, and there was no way an aspiring rocker could escape the influence of Korner's group. The British 'trad jazz' movement had given away to a big blues movement; to put it simply, white kids in the cities were discovering black music from the States, and they started lining up outside clubs to hear it being played. Encouraged by this growing appreciation for R & B and blues, Eric bought a Kay electric guitar for £100 and practiced endlessly.

Overleaf: A close-cropped Clapton (second from left) and the Yardbirds, 1965. Dismayed by the group's move toward a slick pop sound, Eric left the Yardbirds that year.

Clapton joined his first group, the Roosters, in January 1963. The Roosters lasted only eight or nine months and roughly a dozen gigs; they didn't even have a bass player. R & B was flourishing in the London clubs, so the Roosters dished up numbers by Chuck Berry, Bo Diddley, Lightnin' Slim, Fats Domino, and Little Richard. Eric had a day job laying down floors, and between that and his music, there was little time left for his studies.

Left: Eric in Hyde Park, 1964. Around this time, he began listening to Robert Johnson's *King of the Delta Blues Singers*, Volumes 1 and 2. He explained to *Guitar Player* in 1985 that the Johnson LPs 'cover all of my desires musically. Every angle of expression and emotion is expressed on both of those albums.'

Opposite: Clapton's pre-Cream recordings include the classic *Bluesbreakers* album. *Primal Solos* has live Bluesbreakers tracks with Eric and Jack Bruce.

He would bring his guitar to school and get drunk during lunchtime, eventually causing such a stir that he was kicked out of art school. When the Roosters folded, he and fellow guitarist Tom McGuinness hooked up with a singer named Casey Jones to form the group Casey Jones & the Engineers. Clapton honed his playing on more Chuck Berry tunes, but Jones was a dismal singer and Eric quit after seven gigs. Next stop: the Yardbirds.

The Yardbirds were a scrappy R & B-based group that had inherited the Rolling Stones' spot at the Crawdaddy Club. Lead singer Keith Relf knew Eric from art school, and recruited him in October 1963 to replace guitarist Top Topham. It was clear from the start that the Yardbirds were on to something special with their new member. Though the group was, in the end, written off as a minor-league version of the Stones, Clapton's keen musicianship quickly attracted a following. At every Yardbirds gig, a small crowd would cluster on Eric's side of the stage, mesmerized by every move he made. He picked up the nickname 'Slowhand' because whenever

he broke the strings on his Telecaster (which was often), he would change them onstage to the accompaniment of a slow handclap from the band and the audience. A guitar hero was in the making.

The Yardbirds were soon on their way to the top. By the spring of 1964, the band had backed visiting bluesman Sonny Boy Williamson (an event which was recorded for a live album) and had made several TV appearances. They were packing them in at the Marquee, London's most popular club in the '60s. A *Record Mirror* poll in April ranked the Yardbirds the third best group behind the Stones and Manfred Mann, and that summer, they played a memorable set at Richmond's National Jazz & Blues Festival, further ensuring their swelling popularity.

Clapton's recorded legacy with the Yardbirds consists of the live album with Sonny Boy Williamson, *Five Live Yardbirds*, and several cuts on the hastily packaged *For Your Love* LP. 'I Ain't Got You' lopes along like any early Stones/Hollies/Animals R & B retread, until a raving solo from Clapton strikes like a bolt from out of the blue. On the whole, though, there aren't many early signs of Eric's genius in his Yardbirds recordings. In contrast, some uncanny guitarwork does crop up on Eric's earliest session appearance, two numbers with Otis Spann: 'Calcutta Blues' and 'Pretty Girls Everywhere.' The latter track highlights the kind of fluidity that would quickly become his trademark.

Clapton continued to delve deeper and deeper into the blues, immersing himself in the recordings of the mysterious Robert Johnson. Johnson was the most significant of the Delta bluesmen of the 1930s, writing and recording enduring classics such as 'Crossroads,' 'Love in Vain,' 'Dust My Broom,' and 'Sweet Home Chicago.' Johnson's music, and especially his inscrutable guitar technique, was a powerful influence on a whole generation of blues artists and rockers, black and white, American and British. Clapton, for his part, was awed by the intensity of Johnson's playing, and he struggled to make the music more accessible to young listeners.

While Eric grew more serious about the blues, the Yardbirds started moving away from cover versions of black material and shifting to a lightweight, more commercial formula. For Clapton, the Yardbirds' pop hit 'For Your Love' was the last straw. Disappointed by the way the Yardbirds had veered away from the crude R & B sound captured

Above: John Mayall and his Bluesbreakers incubated a number of British blues players, such as Fleetwood Mac's Peter Green and Mick Taylor of the Rolling Stones.

on *Five Live Yardbirds*, he quit the band and went to the home of ex-Rooster Ben Palmer. Legend has it that he locked himself in a room with just his guitar, forging the style that would blow a hole in the world of rock music and inspire the slogan 'Clapton is God.'

In early 1965, Eric joined John Mayall's Bluesbreakers, showing a startling instrumental prowess even from his earliest club dates with the band. Eric was at first reluctant to dive into another band so soon after leaving the Yardbirds. But John Mayall was a commanding presence on the British blues scene, and Clapton was drawn to his firm leadership and commitment to the blues.

With the Bluesbreakers, Clapton proved that he could not only play like Buddy Guy, Freddie King, and Otis Rush – he could go *beyond* them, melding these influences into his own distinctive style. At that time, most white British blues guitarists played as if politely respectful of their American heroes. When Eric took a solo, though, he sounded aggressive and downright nasty. As producer Mike Vernon told John Pidgeon: 'There were other guitar players around . . . but [Eric] somehow had managed to latch on to the same kind of fire and attack, and the same kind of flowing phrase, that B.B. King and Freddie King were so good at doing. . . . He was the only guitarist at the time who actually latched on to it and was able to relate to it and reproduce it.'

After four months with Mayall, Clapton was itching to try something new: a world tour with the Glands, a free-wheeling and hard-drinking crew of amateur musicians. The trip turned out to be a disaster, with the Glands only getting as far as Greece before Eric returned to Mayall's Bluesbreakers in October 1965. Meanwhile, Jack Bruce, ex-bass player for the Graham Bond Organisation, had temporarily replaced future Fleetwood Mac member John McVie in the group. When Eric played onstage with Jack in the Bluesbreakers, he was impressed by the way this Scotsman, with his intricate bass lines, could stretch out each of the band's numbers, pulling Mayall's music in a looser, jazzier direction. Clapton felt a musical kinship with Jack; after all, Eric's own playing hinted at the rhythmic sensibility of a jazz musician. He and Bruce were in the Bluesbreakers together until December, when Jack quit to join Manfred Mann.

From November 1965 through the spring of 1966, with Eric's guitar solos drawing bigger and bigger crowds to Mayall gigs, 'Clapton is God' graffiti started appearing scrawled on walls all over London. Ads in the music press billed the band as 'John Mayall's Bluesbreakers featuring Eric Clapton.' He cut an enigmatic figure onstage: standing completely still, his eyes tightly shut, a sharply dressed Eric would reel off searing licks as though oblivious to the world outside. He would turn his back to the audience, deep in concentration, while fans shouted for him to keep playing. Like his boyhood heroes, Clapton had finally become that one man with a guitar versus the world.

In March 1966, the Bluesbreakers went into the studio one Saturday afternoon and recorded an LP which has become a Clapton classic: *John Mayall's Bluesbreakers with Eric Clapton*. Live tracks of the Bluesbreakers that surfaced years later on John Mayall's *Primal Cuts* prove that the *Bluesbreakers* album – unlike many of Eric's later efforts – succeeded in capturing the intensity of his live work. One reason is Eric's insistence on playing his Gibson Les Paul at full volume in the studio. 'He had a terrible time with the engineer,' drummer Hughie Flint recalled to John Pidgeon, 'because he wanted his amp up, and [the engineer] was tearing his hair out, "You turn down, we'll do it in here," and Eric said, "No, I can't play unless I play like I play on stage."' The result is a thick, high-sustain tone – and some of the most powerful blues guitar that Eric has ever committed to vinyl.

John Mayall's Bluesbreakers with Eric Clapton, which appeared in the summer of 1966, had a huge effect on other British musicians, spawning a host of Clapton imitators. Freddie King's 'Hideaway,' Otis Rush's 'All Your Love,' and Robert Johnson's 'Ramblin' on My Mind' (with Eric's first recorded lead vocal) pointed to Eric's major guitar influences. His solos on instrumental features like 'Steppin' Out' and 'Hideaway,' as well as on numbers like 'Double Crossing Time' and 'Have You Heard', have a savage authority all their own. In short, even if Clapton had never played another note in his life, the *Bluesbreakers* album would undoubtedly have assured him a place in rock history.

Amazingly enough for a blues album, *John Mayall's Bluesbreakers with Eric Clapton* climbed into the British Top Ten three weeks after its release, and remained there for another two months. Over in the States, the Paul Butterfield Band's *East-West* album raised the stakes in the white-blues-guitar game (though Eric later noted that he didn't much care for Mike Bloomfield's undisciplined riffing). But Clapton had already picked up his marbles and moved on to join a new group. He had become weary of Mayall's by-the-book blues, and as he would do throughout his career, he moved on to something more stimulating. Jack Bruce's adventurous bass playing, combined with Ginger Baker's jazzy drumming, would offer him a new outlet. He didn't quite know what they would play together, though – and he didn't quite suspect that Cream would turn out to be the ultimate musical challenge.

Above: Eric performing with Cream on British TV's 'Ready, Steady, Go' in 1966. Note the Gibson Les Paul, which Clapton played at Bluesbreakers gigs.

Sitting on Top of the World – Cream

When Eric Clapton joined forces with Jack Bruce and Ginger Baker to form Cream, not one of them had a clear concept of what kind of music they would be playing. Eric described his original fantasy to Ray Coleman: 'I would be the slick front man, the Buddy Guy type, a white Buddy Guy, the guy with the big suit, baggy trousers, doing straight blues. The other two would be the perfect back up. . . . When we had our first rehearsal, that just went completely out the window.'

Clapton knew drummer Ginger Baker from sitting in with the Graham Bond Organisation. After Baker guested with the Bluesbreakers at a gig in Oxford, he approached Eric with the idea of forming a group. Clapton said yes, but only if they could get Jack Bruce as a bass player. Jack and Ginger were hardly good buddies, since Baker had fired Bruce from Graham Bond's outfit six months earlier. The two had engaged in frequent onstage fistfights, and even in Cream, they never really got along with each other. But as often happens with musicians, this antagonism made for a top-notch rhythm section.

Previous pages: A rather mind-bending photo of Cream in 1967, with Clapton in sunglasses.

Below: Ginger Baker (drums), Eric Clapton (guitar), Jack Bruce (bass) – Cream.

At the end of June 1966, the British music-trade paper, *Melody Maker*, announced the formation of 'a sensational new groups' group' and reported that Cream (a name that alluded to these players being the 'cream of the crop') had signed with Robert Stigwood's Reaction label. According to *Melody Maker*, the band would debut in July at the Windsor Jazz & Blues Festival, at which time their first single would be released. Cream was an unusual concept. Usually, groups would start out playing local dives, a star would emerge, the 'name' player would leave, then an unknown would be drafted as a replacement. Cream, on the other hand, began with three established stars.

The music press wondered how the jazz backgrounds of Bruce and Baker would mix with Clapton's blues purism in this supergroup. During rehearsals, when asked to describe what kind of music Cream would be playing, Eric coyly replied 'blues, ancient and modern,' then added, prompted by Bruce, 'sweet and sour rock and roll.' The threesome asserted that the point was to play with and for each other – what they actually played would be an afterthought. Denying that their music would be jazzy, Clapton declared to *Melody Maker* that 'what we want to do is anything that people haven't done before.'

Cream's debut at the Windsor festival drew an ecstatic reaction, with 10,000 fans standing ankle-deep in mud and screaming for Eric to play more, even as he was soloing. Jack hammered on a Fender six-string bass and Ginger thundered away behind a seven-

Above and right: From the moment they started rehearsing together, these three musicians knew they were onto something special. After the band's first gig at the Windsor Jazz & Blues Festival in 1966, *Melody Maker* assessed: 'Although the Cream are still in the experimental stage, they are striving for a perfection which, when it does come, will be little short of sensational.'

Above: 'Are we on yet?' Cream prepare for an early appearance on the British show 'Ready, Steady, Go.'

piece, double-bass-drum set (Baker was the first rock drummer to use so much equipment). They were still in an experimental stage, though, padding some of their songs with improvisation because they had so little rehearsed material to perform.

The trio recorded *Fresh Cream* in September 1966, and the next month, the long-awaited single appeared. 'Wrapping Paper' was a bizarre track, nothing like the music Cream was playing live. There were no solos, and this pleasant but trifling soft-shoe ditty seemed to imply that Cream would not be Clapton plus back-up musicians. The 'B' side, 'Cat's Squirrel,' was a much more tantalizing taste of what was to come.

Fresh Cream, released in December, set Cream's style – riff-based song structures that would allow for extended improvisation. The album mixed original material with classic blues numbers like Willie Dixon's 'Spoonful,' Robert Johnson's 'From Four Until Late,' Muddy Waters' 'Rollin' And Tumblin',' and Skip James's 'I'm So Glad.' Bruce wrote most of the original songs, collaborating with poet/musician Pete Brown on several; the balance came from Baker and his wife, Janet Godfrey.

Below: Bruce and Clapton. Whereas most electric bassists use 4-stringed instruments, Jack played a 6-string bass.

Overleaf: Wedding jazz improvisation to a thunderous rock sound, Cream forged an early version of the 'heavy metal' style.

The most striking feature of *Fresh Cream* is the extraordinary empathy between the musicians, and the fact that the sound was created by only three players. Clapton may have walked into Cream as strictly a blues player, but Bruce's jazzy bass figures and Baker's relentless drumming were already forcing him into new territory. 'I Feel Free' sported an almost off-key solo from Eric; 'Sweet Wine,' laced with howling feedback, had him spitting out piercing notes. 'Sleepy Time Time' was a bluesy vehicle that highlighted Clapton's sweet-toned stringbending; 'Spoonful' was built like a John Mayall number, with a furious guitar outburst from Eric. All in all, it was an exciting first album.

By the time *Fresh Cream* came out, Cream had taken big strides beyond the music represented on the LP. To Eric, Jack, and Ginger, *Fresh Cream* was not too fresh. And the limited extent of the group's ties to the blues was clear from their British club tour in the fall of 1966. Apart from isolated numbers like 'Lawdy Mama,' 'The First Time I Met the Blues,' 'Steppin' Out,' and occasionally 'Hideaway,' Cream rarely featured straight-ahead Chicago blues. After seeing Jimi Hendrix in London, Eric wanted to explore a new type of guitar playing, a style that might de-emphasize the blues. At the same time, a split was developing between Cream's tightly knit songs on record and the unfettered, anything-goes feel of their live performances.

Ludwig
GINGER
Drum City
Ludwig
BAKER
Drum City

Above: Jimi Hendrix, who appeared with Cream in October 1966, exerted a huge influence on Eric's guitarwork.

After a European tour in early 1967, Cream visited America to play a Murray the K show at New York's RKO Theatre for 10 days. The curtain went up at 10:00 in the morning on a crassly commercial affair that packaged a host of bands like the Who, the Lovin' Spoonful, Mitch Ryder, Simon & Garfunkel, and Wilson Pickett. For Cream, as road manager Ben Palmer recalled to John Pidgeon, it was '['I'm So Glad'] five times a day, it had to be the same, had to have the same quote from the "Marseillaise," shouldn't necessarily go over three minutes' – all for shrieking teenyboppers who wanted them to smash up their equipment like the Who.

Clapton, Bruce, and Baker had counted on coming to the States and being taken seriously as musicians. They were so dismayed by the tackiness of the Murray the K deal that arrangements were made for Cream to record their second album at Atlantic Studios in April 1967. Luckily, while in New York, the group got to jam at the Cafe Au Go Go in Greenwich Village, sitting in with the Blues Project's Al Kooper and Steve Katz, the Mothers of Invention, and Mitch Ryder. Eric enjoyed the heady creative atmosphere and the Village nightlife, absorbing a slew of musical influences.

The band's next album, *Disraeli Gears*, introduced Cream to engineering whiz Tom Dowd and eight-track recording. Having lost his sunburst Gibson Les Paul to a thief in late 1966, Eric was now playing a 1961 SG-shaped Les Paul with a psychedelic paint job. More so than on *Fresh Cream*, his guitarwork on the LP's quirky songs showed a dazzling breadth of expression. He spent a great deal of time in the studio overdubbing guitar parts, weaving sinuous, swirling lines on 'World of Pain' and mimicking 'sirens sweetly singing' on 'Tales of Brave Ulysses.' *Disraeli Gears* also featured a lyrical guitar sound dubbed 'woman tone,' which Eric achieved by rolling back the tone controls and cranking the volume full up. On 'Tales of Brave Ulysses,' Clapton played with a wah-wah pedal; Hendrix, who was a big influence on Eric's playing at this period and who had used wah-wah on his 'Burning of the Midnight Lamp,' had given him the device to cry out.

Unlike Cream's first album, *Disraeli Gears* had no direct cover versions. Clapton started appearing in the songwriting credits, as did Felix Pappalardi and his wife as well as Australian artist Martin Sharp (who designed the wild record sleeve). 'Strange Brew,' adapted from an old live Cream number ('Lawdy

Mama') and sung by Eric, acknowledged one of Clapton's major guitar influences: Albert King. (This electric bluesman's gravelly voice and manic stringbending, captured on early-'60s recordings for the Stax label, made a strong impression on musicians like Jimi Hendrix, Johnny Winter, and Mike Bloomfield.) 'Sunshine of Your Love,' a hit single, had a lilting solo from Clapton and introduced the bottom-heavy riff into the vocabulary of rock guitar; 'Dance the Night Away' sounded like a San Francisco-influenced tribute to the Byrds. Unfortunately, 'Blue Condition,' Baker's plodding contribution to the album, was no 'Sweet Wine.'

More importantly, except for 'Outside Woman Blues' and 'Take It Back,' there was not much blues in evidence on *Disraeli Gears*. Eric was too busy crafting a revolutionary approach to the electric guitar within Jack Bruce's pop-flavored framework. In mid-1967, he told *Rolling Stone*: 'I don't think I really represent the blues anymore. Not truly. I have more of that in me and my music than anything else but I don't really play blues anymore.' Yet try as he might to push beyond the blues format – by improvising at high volume and coloring the sound of his instrument with electronic effects – Clapton seemed to play with the most conviction whenever he retapped his blues roots.

Though *Disraeli Gears* did not hit the record racks until November 1967, two tracks – 'Strange Brew' and 'Tales of Brave Ulysses'

Below: Scotsman Bruce and Irishman Baker both played jazz in the Graham Bond Organisation before joining forces with Clapton in Cream.

Left: Day-Glo album covers, surrealistic song lyrics, and wild outfits contributed to an early psychedelic image for the group.

Right: While with Cream, Eric began forsaking blue jeans and work shirts for more exotic garb.

– were pulled and issued as a single at the beginning of June. The members of Cream returned to England and pondered their accomplishments to date. Their gigs that summer attracted rave reviews, but they were still basically a ballroom-and-club band, with one disappointing American visit behind them, only moderate chart success, and no hope that another tour of the States would be any different.

The turning point for Cream came at San Francisco's Fillmore West in August 1967. The house was packed night after night, convincing the band that it had underestimated Cream's American following. The way the three played together changed to suit their appreciative fans. Jack Bruce explained to *Guitar Player*: 'We played the Fillmore, and prior to that time, we did . . . three- and five-minute versions [of the songs]. But when we got to San Francisco, there was such a loose feeling about the whole time. . . . We went through a couple of short songs, and the audience was shouting out, "Just play!" So we started to improvise, to lengthen the solos, and go along with the feeling.'

Cream onstage was quite a sight – and sound – to behold. The 50-watt Marshall amp and 4 × 12 speaker cabinets of Clapton's Mayall days had given away to a 100-watt triple stack. The spectacle of three virtuosos goading each other onstage to improvisational heights was new to rock audiences. With a minimum of showmanship, Eric, Jack, and Ginger would generate a wall of sound, continually pushing and pulling each other. Cream's live recordings reveal how each player sounded as if he was soloing; at the same time, they were all swapping musical phrases. Musicians playing as much for each other as for the audience was commonplace in jazz, but no group before Cream had ever attempted it in a rock setting.

Cream returned to England as conquering heros, to play a string of club dates. Readers of *Melody Maker*, in their annual popularity poll, voted Clapton Musician of the Year. But the strain produced by that popularity, plus their over-indulgent playing, became glaringly manifest. At one Wembley concert, Jack Bruce walked offstage halfway through the set, leaving Eric and Ginger to finish up. (Clapton later mentioned how he once stopped playing during a number, and the other two didn't even notice.) The threesome traveled separately and would stay in different hotels, only seeing each other five minutes before the show. The bickering between Bruce and Baker, which had been going on from the very beginning, got worse; Clapton, caught in the crossfire of two men who intensely disliked one another, was sometimes reduced to tears.

One telling gesture occurred at London's Saville Theatre in January 1968. Eric hoisted his guitar onto some chains and swung it back and forth to get feedback. Such an empty theatrical move could only mean one thing: the pop-star status was going to Clapton's head. 'When Cream became acknowledged as virtuosos,' he told Ray Coleman, 'that's when the rot set in, because *we* started to believe it, and became very cynical about success.'

Nonetheless, the Fillmore experience made it clear that Cream could clean up in America. In February 1968, they kicked off a grueling U.S. tour which turned out to be the longest American tour by a British act to date. Their set at this time usually ran like so: 'Tales of Brave Ulysses,' 'Sunshine of Your Love,'

Above: In London's Soho, 1967.

'NSU,' 'Sitting on Top of the World,' 'Traintime,' 'Toad.' Some numbers were really open-ended excuses for jamming and others were solo showcases; on a good night, the trio could be endlessly inventive. But often, each player would thrash out his own musical ideas with little regard for what the others were doing ('NSU' on *Live Cream* is a case in point). Also, with no time to write or rehearse new material on the road, Clapton, Bruce, and Baker had to play the same songs night after night – a situation bound to exhaust the creativity of even the most gifted musician.

From August 1967 through July 1968, Cream was on top of the world, having moved from cult band to superstar attraction. *Disraeli Gears* and 'Sunshine of Your Love' happened to catch young audiences at the perfect time. Such albums as the Beatles' *Sgt. Pepper's Lonely Hearts Club Band*, Jimi Hendrix's *Are You Experienced*, the Doors' self-titled first album, and Jefferson Airplane's *Surrealistic Pillow* were rapidly changing the shape of rock music in the States. With its Day-Glo cover art and cryptic lyrics, *Disraeli Gears* rode the crest of 'Summer of Love' psychedelia. In San Francisco, such groups as the Airplane, Quicksilver Messenger Service, and the Grateful Dead were threading their feedback-drenched music through meandering twists and turns; at one of these concerts, a song could run anywhere from ten minutes to an hour long. Clapton summed up the contemporary approach to live playing when he explained to Ray Coleman, 'We started on a theme and improvised on it, and because there were only three people, as long as we got back to the same place in the tune at the same time, it was okay.'

In May 1968, *Melody Maker* reported that Cream would tour England upon its return from America in July. But after the group finished its U.S. tour in June, manager Robert Stigwood announced that Cream would disband at the end of the year. Cream would do a farewell tour of the States and play one engagement at London's Royal Albert Hall. Stigwood stressed to *Melody Maker* that the break was amicable, that the three were splitting up to 'follow their individual musical policies.'

Clapton had been yearning for a more flexible format than Cream's power trio. What really turned his head were the tapes he heard of the Band's *Music from Big Pink*, a song-oriented album that relied more on keyboard textures than bravura soloing. Upon listening to the tapes, Clapton later admitted to Ray Coleman, 'I realized we were already out of date and there was no way of trying to get the other two to move forward. . . . I felt I wanted to change Cream but it wasn't up to me. I wasn't the leader of the band . . . That's why I faced up to a split.'

A few weeks after the news of Cream's demise, *Wheels of Fire* appeared. The double album, which consisted of one studio LP and one live disk recorded at the Fillmore West, went gold in the U.S. before it was even shipped. The studio material was solid overall, though there were no Clapton songs; he barely sang at all, and Jack Bruce was clearly the leader. Howlin' Wolf's 'Sitting on Top of the World' and Albert King's 'Born Under a Bad Sign,' two blues numbers, were apparently Eric's ideas. Ironically, his solos on these tracks, which substituted a tougher sound for the 'woman tone' of *Disraeli Gears*, were not very inspired. His work on 'White Room' (with superb wah-wah playing), 'Politician,' 'Deserted Cities of the Heart,' and 'Those Were the Days' was much more fiery.

With a studio half and a live half, *Wheels of Fire* depicted Cream as two very different bands. 'Spoonful,' a centerpiece of their shows, epitomizes the best and the worst aspects of Cream in concert – the central theme is so thin that you can hear the trio lurching from one transition to another, with Clapton struggling to keep up. But if there is any song that is Cream in a nutshell, it is 'Crossroads,' perhaps the pinnacle of Clapton's achievement with the group. This Robert Johnson number, thanks to liquid phrasing from Eric and supple support from Bruce and Baker, has become a rock-guitar classic. Years later, engineer Tom Dowd spilled the beans: Clapton's demonic solos seem concise only because Dowd edited the track down from a longer performance.

Before Cream's final U.S. tour, Eric made one of his most memorable session appearances with some gorgeous guitarwork on the Beatles' 'While My Guitar Gently Weeps.' This guest spot came about as a result of the close musical and personal relationship that Clapton had developed with George Harrison. His solo is a mini-jewel, packing a maxi-

Right: Jack's bass – and Eric's 1961 SG-shaped Les Paul – were custom-painted by a pair of Dutch designers known as The Fool.

Below: Cream's final performance, at London's Royal Albert Hall on 26 November 1968. The second show is available on home video as *Cream's Farewell Concert*.

Above: Cream's albums were incredibly successful: *Disraeli Gears* stayed on Billboard's best-selling albums chart for 50 weeks, and *Wheels of Fire* even hit number one.

Opposite: 'But the rainbow has a beard' – Ginger, crown prince of percussion, summoning the muse of acid rock.

mum of melodic expressiveness into a short space of time. Eric was already headed in a new direction, for this was nothing like his pyrotechnics with Cream.

Cream's six-week American tour, which started in October 1968, earned Clapton, Bruce, and Baker $650,000. For the farewell concert at the Royal Albert Hall, a second show was added when the first one sold out in two hours. (This second show was taped for BBC broadcast and released as *Cream's Farewell Concert*.) The huge response from British fans made the band reconsider breaking up – but it was too late. The magic was gone.

There was, though, another album. *Goodbye* was wrapped up in December and came out in March 1969. Like *Wheels of Fire*, it was part-live, part-studio. The live cuts had some imaginative interplay between the threesome; on 'Sitting on Top of the World,' Eric pulls wailing blues licks from his Bluesbreakers bag, ending the song with a defiantly flashy riff. For *Goodbye*, each member of the group contributed his own studio tracks. Clapton's 'Badge' – co-written with George Harrison, and featuring the Beatle on rhythm guitar – showed the undeniable influence of the Band, and has since become part of Eric's live repertoire. The track was very short by Cream standards, with an economical solo, plus piano and mellotron fleshing out the trio sound. And not surprisingly, the guitar part during the bridge in 'Badge' – played through a rotating Leslie speaker – sounds a lot like Robbie Robertson on the Band's *Music from Big Pink*.

After the break-up, Clapton, Bruce, and Baker found it hard to live down the reputations they acquired as members of Cream. Everything they did afterwards was compared to their work in the band. Interviewers constantly asked them about Cream, and promoters offered them big sums to reunite. Over the years, their record company kept the flame alive by repackaging Cream leftovers. Still, all the talk of Cream reuniting was useless. For in the end, once Eric, Jack, and Ginger stopped playing for each other, there was no reason to play together at all.

Can’t Find My Way Home — Blind

Faith, Delaney & Bonnie, and Solo

Having reached the apex of rock stardom with Cream, the 23-year-old Clapton needed a chance to decompress. He bought an old mansion called Hurtwood Edge in the English countryside and retreated there, keeping a low profile from December 1968 through February 1969. He did venture out for the Rolling Stones' 'Rock and Roll Circus,' a two-day extravaganza filmed for TV but unreleased to this day. There was also an overblown supersession at an abandoned warehouse in Staines, England, filmed and available on video as *Supershow*. Jamming with a line-up of jazz-rock musicians, Clapton seemed a bit out of his depth, but turned in a crazed solo on one instrumental called 'Slate 69.'

In December 1968, Traffic – a British group that garnered critical notice with its stylish blend of folk, R & B, and jazz – had disbanded. That left Steve Winwood, the group's keyboardist and co-founder, free of any commitments. Eric had wanted to collaborate with Winwood ever since the early '60s, when he first heard of this whiz kid who could do a superb Ray Charles imitation. Later, the two of them would meet and jam together (Steve could also play bass, guitar, and drums). One such get-together was a one-off recording session with Powerhouse, a group that consisted of Ben Palmer (piano), Jack Bruce (bass), Pete York (drums), Paul Jones (harmonica), and Winwood on vocals and organ. The three resulting tracks – issued on the Elektra sampler *What's Shakin'*, and including an early version of 'Crossroads' – were ragged and forgettable, with little chemistry between Eric and Steve in evidence.

But something magical happened during Christmas of 1968, when Winwood stayed with Clapton at Hurtwood Edge and the duo jammed for hours on end. Eric explained to Steve that he was tired of the superstar bit, that he wanted to focus more on songs, not overblown solos. But no sooner did he outline some vague ideas to *Melody Maker* about

Pages 38-39: Steve Winwood, Rick Grech, and Ginger Baker teamed up with Eric in the short-lived group Blind Faith.

Opposite top: Clapton jamming with Keith Richards (on bass) and John Lennon at the Rolling Stones' Rock & Roll Circus, December 1968.

Opposite bottom: A pensive Eric in 1970, attempting to wind down from his superstar days with Cream.

Above: Even more so than Cream, Blind Faith was touted by the press as a supergroup – but the band imploded after one album and a nightmarish American tour.

joining forces with Winwood than the music press began speculating how great a Clapton-Winwood band could be. All the while, Eric tried to downplay the rumors about a supergroup along the lines of Cream. The plan was to find a drummer and play as a trio; as Clapton and Winwood started the search, Ginger Baker dropped by Steve's house and offered his services. Steve talked a reluctant Eric into having Ginger join; with Baker on board, it was now impossible to avoid the 'supergroup' tag.

In the early months of 1969, the still-unnamed outfit did some recording in Olympic Studios, while the music press announced that the group would tour Scandinavia and make its British debut at a free concert in London's Hyde Park on June 7. Eric insisted that the band would be totally different from Cream, and characterized Winwood as the focal point and *de facto* bandleader. 'Blind Faith,' the group's name, seemed to mock the expectations of fans – expectations that were being pumped up daily by the British pop press. Rick Grech, a bassist who had been in the group Family, joined Clapton, Baker, and Winwood in the studio to help record what would be the *Blind Faith* LP.

Unfortunately, one solid album and a dreadful American tour is all that Blind Faith left behind. What did the group in was the pressure from management and the record company to make big money. *Melody Maker* noted even before the band's debut that concert offers for Blind Faith were topping Cream's figures; the asking price per concert was $20,000 against percentages of gate receipts. Also, since Clapton and company were being hustled onstage, they had no time to write enough material, so that the concept behind Blind Faith as a live act was fragile from the start. 'There were pressures left, right and center to go out and earn the money,' Steve Winwood told Ray Coleman. 'Never was there a moment to develop the character of the band . . . when it came down to it, we failed because we couldn't resist requests for the hits. Ginger did a drum solo and they thought it was Cream, so we chucked in an old Cream song ['Crossroads'], then I put in a Traffic song ['Means to an End'], and the identity of the band was killed stone dead.'

Blind Faith's much-ballyhooed appearance at Hyde Park – in front of a crowd estimated at 150,000 – was a disappointment.

Left: Clapton practicing on a Gibson ES-335, which he played at Cream's farewell concert.

Right: Eric in 1969, after the breakup of Blind Faith and before joining Delaney & Bonnie.

The concert seemed, as one *Melody Maker* wrote, 'very much like Steve Winwood plus a backing group.' Blind Faith was woefully underrehearsed, and it showed. The playing was casual, with only Ginger Baker attempting to create sparks. It was to little avail – there was no Cream-like rapport between the musicians.

After a short Scandinavian jaunt, Blind Faith invaded America, kicking off a summer tour in Newport, Rhode Island. The warm-up act was Delaney & Bonnie, a husband-and-wife duo that Eric had first seen in his Cream days. On the recommendation of George Harrison, Blind Faith featured Delaney & Bonnie on their tour, a decision that would have weighty consequences for Clapton's career.

The U.S. tour was an unqualified disaster, with Clapton feeling trapped in an embarassing situation from day one. The sound at most of the shows was atrocious, and the revolving stage didn't help matters. At Madison Square Garden, after shelling out high prices for a barely audible 90-minute show, disgruntled fans rioted for 45 minutes. A concert at the L.A. Forum typified the kind of violence that hounded the group across America: the house lights had to be turned on repeatedly as the police dragged fans from the auditorium, and security guards jumped onstage, pushing Clapton back towards the amplifiers. Winwood, disgusted with the whole scene, complained to *Musician Player and Listener* of the crowds' 'mindless adulation, mostly due to Eric and Ginger's success with Cream.' One audience gave Blind Faith a standing ovation before the group had even played a single note.

In the midst of this chaos, the *Blind Faith* album appeared in August 1969. With advance orders of half a million copies, *Blind Faith* quickly rocketed to the Number One spot on British and American album charts. The controversial cover featured a topless 11-year-old girl, so Atco had to release the album with a different jacket in the U.S. The music? Just as Clapton had indicated, Steve Winwood was the focal point. He did all the lead vocals and wrote three of the six songs; the sound had a Traffic-like feel, except for Baker's heavier drumming style. Maybe the reason Blind Faith seems more like a collection of sketches than a cohesive work is because the group could not produce the album themselves, and had to call in an outside producer to rush the project through.

From the Clapton fan's point of view, *Blind Faith* has some fine guitarwork, but not a great deal. He duels effectively with Winwood on 'Had to Cry Today,' does some delicate picking on 'Can't Find My Way Home,' and pulls off a startling wah-wah break on 'Presence of the Lord,' Clapton's sole contribution to the album. Compared to his high-voltage soloing with Cream, Eric's playing was more in the vein of 'Badge' or 'While My Guitar Gently Weeps': sophisticated and mature. 'If you can be more economical when you play,' he explained to *Melody Maker* at the time, 'you get a chance to be able to see where you can voice things and put things in, rather than just playing full out all the time.' These words reflect the philosophy behind Clapton's first solo album – and, in fact, foreshadow the approach he would take with his entire solo career.

Blind Faith never officially disbanded, but after the American tour, the group slipped back to England and everyone went his separate way. Talk of a British tour and second album came to nothing, and the unspoken consensus was that the group was finished. Eric, for his part, couldn't care less.

Above: Clapton's post-Cream projects – *Blind Faith, Eric Clapton*, and a live album with Delaney & Bonnie – downplayed high-volume guitarwork.

Resentful of the way Ginger Baker had turned his casual jams with Steve Winwood into a sideshow, Clapton had been looking for a way out from the moment Blind Faith hit the road. It came in the form of Blind Faith's warm-up act: Delaney & Bonnie. As road manager Ben Palmer told John Pidgeon, 'Once [Eric] began to spend as much time with them as he did on tour, his whole interest in Blind Faith evaporated almost overnight.'

Delaney Bramlett hailed from Mississippi, and Bonnie Lynn came from Illinois. After recording one album for Stax in 1968, the twosome assembled a remarkable group of players – including Carl Radle, Bobby Whitlock, Jim Keltner, Bobby Keys, and Jim Price – for *Accept No Substitute*, a fusion of rock, soul, and gospel that was way ahead of its time. The word about Delaney & Bonnie quickly spread among West Coast rock musicians, with Hendrix, Mick Jagger, Dr. John, and Stephen Stills soon trumpeting the couple's virtues.

Clapton's special relationship with Delaney & Bonnie evolved after Blind Faith's nightmarish Madison Square Garden gig. The group fled back to England except for Eric, who stayed in New York and hung around with Delaney. He was charmed by these brash, colorful characters and became infatuated with their brand of heartfelt, R & B-inflected sound. Here, after all the supergroup hoopla, were two sincere, unpretentious performers. As he spent more time with Delaney & Bonnie, Clapton found a musical soulmate in Delaney Bramlett. They shared a passion for black bluesmen like Robert Johnson, and Delaney kept at Eric to sing more. Eric resolved to bring Delaney & Bonnie over to England to tour small venues – with himself playing lead guitar.

In the interim, Clapton kept busy after the break-up of Blind Faith. John Lennon asked him at the last minute to join him for a set at the Toronto Rock Festival; they rehearsed on the plane ride over. Lennon's *Live Peace at Toronto* captures Eric furiously riffing on a batch of oldies from John's Beatle days, taking a blinding solo on 'Yer Blues.' Clapton also played on Lennon's studio version of 'Cold Turkey'; guested with the Plastic Ono Band at a UNICEF benefit concert; and participated in some abortive recording sessions with George Harrison, Rick Grech, and Denny Laine.

In November 1969, Delaney & Bonnie came to Hurtwood Edge to rehearse for a low-key British tour that would be billed as 'Delaney & Bonnie and Friends with Eric Clapton.' Soured by the Blind Faith fiasco, Eric was anxious to play the sideman, out of the spotlight. But as usual, publicists and pro-

moters would not let him hide. For the opening concert, the band was 'mistakenly' advertised so that audiences thought that Clapton would be doing a solo set; when that turned out not to be the case, Delaney & Bonnie were booed off the stage after four songs. The rest of the tour, though, came off without a hitch, and Dave Mason and George Harrison even joined in for some shows. Eric clearly relished his role as just one of the guys, and loved the down-home, back-to-the-basics simplicity of traveling by bus. The live *On Tour with Eric Clapton* album documents Delaney & Bonnie's good time soul antics. Sadly for Clapton's fans, Eric's lead-guitar lines are nearly inaudible.

The most important fruit of Clapton's association with Delaney & Bonnie was his first solo album, *Eric Clapton*. Recorded in early 1970, the LP bore the unmistakable stamp of the Delaney & Bonnie style. That's hardly surprising, considering that Delaney wrote eight of the eleven tracks, producing and arranging the album as well. Fans and critics, expecting guitar fireworks from Eric, were disappointed by the Bramlett influence, and faulted *Eric Clapton* for its blandness. *Melody Maker* complained that Eric had 'submerged himself . . . to the point where it really does become a Delaney & Bonnie album featuring E. Clapton (guitar).'

Above: As the opening act for Blind Faith, Delaney & Bonnie enchanted Eric (far right) with their Southern-roots music and unpretentious ways. Clapton enjoyed relative anonymity with the band, and produced his first solo album with its assistance.

In hindsight, and now that Clapton has carved out a viable solo career, the criticisms were unfair. *Eric Clapton* was another instance of the guitarist bucking the trend. At a time when groups like Led Zeppelin and Deep Purple were popularizing the heavy sound he had pioneered with Cream, Eric took a musically honest, straightforward tack for his first solo album. The LP featured some strong songs from Clapton and Delaney; J.J. Cale's 'After Midnight,' a hit single, has even become a kind of signature song for Eric (especially when reworked in 1987 for a Michelob commercial). If his guitar playing was understated, Clapton's singing, thanks to Delaney's encouragement, was confident and exuberant throughout. Also, he had switched from the Gibson Les Paul, with its piercing tone, to a Fender Stratocaster. The result was the tight, beefy sound typical of Eric's latter-day work.

With the wistful 'Easy Now,' the soulful 'Blues Power' (co-written by Leon Russell), and the chiming 'Let It Rain,' *Eric Clapton* showed for the first time that the guitar hero could also be a singer/songwriter. As Eric explained to the music press, the album represented his first step toward becoming a more well-rounded musician. And as his work with Derek & the Dominos would prove, *Eric Clapton* was a step worth taking.

Why Does Love Got to Be So Sad – Derek & the Dominos and the Rainbow Concert

Clapton returned to England in 1970 after a short American tour with Delaney & Bonnie and plunged into heavy session work in London. He played on albums by Howlin' Wolf (the incandescent *London Howlin' Wolf Sessions* showcased Eric's blues work), Steve Stills, and Dr. John. He also invited some ex-Delaney & Bonnie sidemen to his country home to join him as the 'house band' for George Harrison's *All Things Must Pass* album. After jamming incessantly with drummer Jim Gordon, bassist Carl Radle, and keyboardist Bobby Whitlock, Clapton was certain that he had the makings of a group he could call his own. They wouldn't blast him into the stratosphere like Jack Bruce and Ginger Baker did, but they could give him a supple backdrop and let him slowly develop his ideas. In short, the time was ripe for Eric to step out as a bandleader and call the shots.

The empathy that quickly developed between Clapton and the other musicians is clear from the jams that recently surfaced as part of the *Layla Sessions* package. In June 1970, the band debuted as Derek & the Dominos at a Civil Liberties benefit, with Eric leading his crew through songs from the *Eric Clapton* LP and throwing in the occasional crowd-pleaser like 'Crossroads.' Dave Mason played at the gig and was supposed to be a full-fledged Domino, but eventually dropped out to pursue a solo career in the United States.

In the fall of 1970, Derek & the Dominos hit the road for the kind of tour Eric had been dreaming of since his Blind Faith days – small-scale, and in intimate venues like ballrooms and clubs. He wanted the Dominos to perform like any other lads succeeding or failing on their own merits, not being judged as another Clapton project. The plan was that British audiences would not even know that this was Eric's group. They pulled it off in England and got good reviews, but it didn't quite work that way in the States. During an

Previous pages: The Rainbow Concert, with (left to right) Steve Winwood, Ron Wood, Rick Grech, Jimmy Karstein, Clapton, and Pete Townshend.

Below: Clapton hijacked Delaney & Bonnie's sidemen – Jim Gordon (drums), Carl Radle (bass), and Bobby Whitlock (keyboards/vocals) – for his own group, Derek & the Dominos.

Opposite: While recording his first solo album, Eric did a brief U.S. tour with Delaney & Bonnie. Carl Radle (right) was a member of Eric's band through 1979.

Above: Clapton's recorded output between 1970 and 1974 was quite sparse. *Layla* was recently reissued on CD with previously-unreleased alternate takes and jams.

Opposite top: 'Derek' at the Capitol Theater in Port Chester, New York, 4 December 1970.

Opposite bottom: George Harrison with wife Patti, March 1969. The Beatle and Clapton met in 1963, later developing a close musical kinship. Eric's unrequited love for Patti inspired his masterpiece, 'Layla.'

American tour, DEREK IS ERIC buttons were showered on the masses, probably in response to the half-filled stadiums and arenas across the country. Before that, however, Derek & the Dominos interrupted their British tour to fly to Miami's Criteria Studios and record an album with producer Tom Dowd. *Layla and Other Assorted Love Songs* was to be the highlight of Clapton's career.

The Dominos had already cut a hyped-up version of 'Tell the Truth,' with Phil Spector producing, during spare studio time at the *All Things Must Pass* sessions. It was supposed to be released as a single, but at the last minute, it was pulled and 'After Midnight/ Easy Now' from *Eric Clapton* was rushed out instead. Why? After hearing the rendition of 'Tell the Truth' that would eventually make it onto the *Layla* album, the band disapproved of the first version. The original 'Tell the Truth' later turned up on the *History of Eric Clapton* compilation.

On *Layla*, all the facets of Clapton's musicianship – his singing, his songwriting, his guitar playing – came together with explosive force. He joined forces with Bobby Whitlock and wrote five of the album's eight original tracks, some of the strongest and most enduring songs that Clapton has ever written. But another key player – and, by Eric's own admission, the catalyst for the whole *Layla* project – was Duane Allman. Clapton had heard Duane play slide guitar on Wilson Pickett's version of 'Hey Jude,' and, as he later confessed to *Melody Maker*, 'it scared the pants off me.'

Allman's appearance on the album came about via Tom Dowd, who at the time was producing the Allman Brothers' second album at Criteria Studios. During the *Layla* sessions, Dowd took Clapton to see an Allman Brothers concert; afterwards, Eric invited Duane back to the studio. When Allman showed up, the duo jammed on blues numbers, trading licks through the night. The relationship was instantly magical. As Dowd explained to John Pidgeon, 'I thought they had a great deal in common. Eric had a healthy respect for what he heard Duane do, while Duane, listening to a Cream LP, would say, "Man, I wish I could play like that dude in Cream." They were almost identical in personality, strong people but very soft-spoken. . . . The chemistry was there.' One listen to 'Mean Old World,' a *Layla* outtake with Clapton and Allman duetting on acoustic guitars, is proof enough.

Layla and Other Assorted Love Songs is a concept album of sorts, inspired by Eric's unrequited love for George Harrison's wife. Partly to make George jealous, Patti Harrison had an affair with Clapton, meeting him several times in secret. She soon changed her mind, though, and returned to Harrison.

Eric was devastated, and stoked by the drugs lying around the studio in Miami, he took solace in the music he knew the best – the blues. Clapton wrung tortured licks from his Fender Stratocaster, playing with the anger of his John Mayall days on work-outs like 'Have You Ever Loved a Woman' and 'Key to the Highway.' On other songs, some of which sounded like Delaney & Bonnie material, he showed a dignified restraint that was closer in spirit to his work on the *Eric Clapton* album. *Layla* may not have the latter's studio crispness, but is all the better for it: the muddy sonic texture gives the whole recording a gritty, back-to-the-roots feel.

The songs on *Layla* evolved in the studio, and were recorded in exactly the same order in which they appear on the album. Allman's soaring slide pushed Clapton to new heights, prompting ferocious guitarwork – like Eric's intro to 'Have You Ever Loved a Woman' – and fiery interplay on 'Keep on Growing' and 'Why Does Love Got to Be So Sad.' Jimi Hendrix's 'Little Wing' perfectly matched the

These pages: Finally fronting a band of his own, Eric brought the Dominos to New York's Fillmore East on 23-24 October 1970. Portions of the show were recorded and appeared on *Derek & The Dominos In Concert* (1973).

album's anguished mood, and was a tip of the hat to one of Eric's musical soulmates.

Layla's centerpiece is, of course, the majestic title track, a howl of pain that has since become a rock classic. Eric wrote 'Layla' to win Patti over, and based it on the ancient Persian tale of Layla and Mashoun. (In this love story, Mashoun falls so hopelessly in love with the object of his desire that he goes mad.) Apparently, the song started life at a much slower tempo and half as long as it is now. Drummer Jim Gordon, Clapton discovered, was sneaking back into the studio after hours to record his own album of love songs; when Eric heard him playing a piano part, he asked if they could use it for 'Layla.' Gordon's delicate coda adds a sense of calm after the storm.

Layla was released in December 1970, while Derek & the Dominos were touring America, minus Duane. For some strange reason, it sank without a trace. Perhaps rock fans didn't know who Derek was, and the

painting on the album cover may have baffled record-buyers. Even stranger was the 'Layla' single's success when it was re-released in mid-1972: Top Ten in the U.S. Whatever the cause, the LP's commercial failure hit Eric hard and fueled his disillusionment. Having exorcized his personal demons with *Layla*, and having picked up a heroin habit along the way, Clapton lost interest in the Dominos.

Derek & the Dominos in Concert was recorded (and poorly at that) during the band's American tour, but didn't see the light of day for three years. The double album documents the peaks and valleys of the Dominos as a live attraction. Maybe *In Concert* was taped on an off night, but without a Duane Allman to bounce ideas off, Eric often sounds lost. The group was playing huge arenas, so maybe Clapton felt like he was on the rock-star treadmill all over again – especially when fans kept screaming his name over and over during his solos. The live LP also shows the Dominos struggling, their inventiveness flagging on some of the jams. Eric could work up a head of steam on the blues numbers, spitting out a flurry of notes on occasion, and Duane did drop by to play two shows. But for the most part, now that Clapton had gotten *Layla* out of his system, there was not much more for him to say.

Page 54: George Harrison and Clapton at the Concert for Bangladesh, New York, August 1971.

Page 55: Eric at the Concert for Bangladesh, clearly enjoying himself.

Above: 'While My Guitar Gently Weeps' at the Bangladesh benefit. Clapton is playing a Gibson Byrdland.

While working on a second album in 1971, Derek & the Dominos split up. There was too much bickering in the studio, and the band's overindulgence in drugs was taking its toll. The tracks from these aborted sessions, which turned up on the *Crossroads* retrospective in 1988, provide a fascinating glimpse of the direction in which Clapton was heading. Taken together, they are a kind of 'missing link' between the *Layla* sessions and the guitarist's subsequent solo work.

On 1 August 1971, Clapton played George Harrison's Concert for Bangladesh; that December, he made a surprise appearance at a Leon Russell concert; and on 13 January 1973, he did two shows at London's Rainbow Theatre. Otherwise, for more than three years, Eric hid in his country home and snorted heroin with his girlfriend, Alice Ormsby-Gore. The poor reception of *Layla*, as well as his rejection by Patti Harrison, pushed him into a downward spiral of addiction. Three other events contributed to Eric's depression, all of them tragic: the sudden deaths of Jimi Hendrix, Duane Allman, and Jack Clapp, Eric's grandfather/adoptive father.

With Clapton in seclusion – refusing to answer his telephone or open his mail – rumors started circulating that he was ill, dead, or addicted to drugs. The record companies kept the product flowing, though, filling the void with *History of Eric Clapton*, two LPs' worth of live Cream, and hastily compiled retrospectives. The music press, often writing about Clapton as if he were dead, cited his seminal role in rock history and praised *Layla* as his unjustly ignored masterpiece. In fact, the guitar hero was so missed during this time that when they were reissued in 1972, the *Layla* album and its title track were runaway successes.

Below: For over three years, Eric holed up in his country house with Alice Ormsby-Gore. The two were engaged in 1969, but never married.

Throughout those years, he and Alice would venture into London quite a bit, and even attend the occasional concert (such as a Who performance in Paris). Clapton passed the time building model airplanes; he played guitar every day, and made tapes. 'I had a box full of cassettes at the end of that period,' he told Ray Coleman. 'There was me, playing guitar, and I hadn't remembered doing them at all.' Eventually, his drug habit grew to consume £1500 a week, forcing him to pawn his guitars for the extra cash.

Below: Clapton's legendary Rainbow Concert (1973) included luminaries such as Rolling Stone-to-be Ron Wood (far left) and the Who's Pete Townshend (far right).

Clapton's 'comeback,' the legendary Rainbow Concert, was orchestrated by the Who's Pete Townshend. In August 1972, Eric asked Townshend over to Hurtwood Edge to help him work on some unfinished Derek & the Dominos tracks. Pete was appalled to hear that his old friend was selling guitars to buy heroin, and dismayed by Eric's low self-esteem. Townshend told Melvyn Bragg, on BBC-TV's 'South Bank Show,' that Clapton spoke of 'want[ing] to be like some of his heroes – deadbeats living out of baked-bean cans in the Delta.' Meanwhile, Lord Harlech (Alice Ormsby-Gore's father) considered staging a musical event to celebrate England's entry into the Common Market on 1 January 1973. Here was the perfect opportunity for Eric to get back on his feet again: two benefit concerts at London's Rainbow Theatre, fronting an all-star band. Townshend had to push him, but Clapton finally agreed to do it.

The supporting cast for Eric Clapton's Rainbow Concert was impressive, to say the least: Pete Townshend (rhythm guitar), Steve Winwood (keyboards), Ron Wood (guitar), Rick Grech (bass), Traffic's Jim Capaldi (drums), and J.J. Cale's Jimmy Karstein (drums). Rehearsals at Ron Wood's house were slapdash, though, and all the players – who feared that Clapton hadn't touched a guitar in years – were jittery enough for Rick Grech to dub the group 'The Palpitations.'

The Rainbow Concert, consisting of an afternoon and an evening show, was a polished, spirited affair. With so many luminaries packed onstage at once, this kind of event can often turn into a messy jam session. Not so in this case: Clapton was the center of attention, and the emphasis was squarely on songs from his solo album and *Layla*. The running order of the set was: 'Layla,' 'Badge,' 'Blues Power,' 'Nobody Knows You When You're Down and Out' (sung by Winwood), 'Roll It Over,' 'Why Does Love Got to Be So Sad,' 'Little Wing,' 'Bottle Of Red Wine,' 'Presence of the Lord,' 'Tell the

Below: Pete Townshend (right) helped organize the Rainbow Concert. Eric told Ray Coleman, 'He gave me faith in myself again.'

Opposite: A barely-recognizable Eric at the Rainbow Concert.

Truth,' Traffic's 'Pearly Queen,' 'Key to the Highway,' 'Let It Rain,' 'Crossroads,' and 'Layla' again as the encore. The first show also featured a menacing version of 'After Midnight,' and 'Bell Bottom Blues.' During 'Let It Rain,' Eric broke a string but continued flailing away, the string swinging from the guitar. On 'Presence of the Lord,' his blistering wah-wah solo broke the effects pedal.

All in all, Eric proved that he could still play a mean guitar. The performances were magnificent, and the critical response was ecstatic. Unfortunately, none of the magic was captured on the poorly recorded sludge later issued as *Eric Clapton's Rainbow Concert.* Because of inadequate miking, most of the instruments (and most of the musical interplay) were completely absent from the recording. And however much the Rainbow Concert may have revived Clapton's self-confidence and restored his reputation, it wasn't really a comeback. Eric shuffled back to Hurtwood Edge and re-cloistered himself there, resuming his heroin habit.

It took Clapton another year before he truly overcame his drug dependency. But when he did, he seemed to rise reborn from the ashes – as a full-fledged solo artist.

Drifting Blues – The Solo Years, Part One

Below right: Robert Stigwood, the Australian rock impresario responsible for *Saturday Night Fever.* Stigwood was Cream's manager, and was Eric's manager until 1979.

Opposite: Clapton at New York's Madison Square Garden, 13 July 1974. At this concert, Todd Rundgren jammed with Eric on Chuck Berry's 'Little Queenie.'

Clapton finally kicked his heroin habit in early 1974 with the help of Dr. Meg Patterson and her 'black box' cure, an electro-acupuncture machine. He did some hard physical labor on a farm in Wales, rebuilding his health, until he was ready to hunker down to a solo career.

Rested and refreshed, Eric asked manager Robert Stigwood to set up some studio time with producer Tom Dowd at Miami's Criteria Studios, the site of the *Layla* sessions. He didn't even have a band, but he did have his old Domino crony, Carl Radle, in mind. Down in Florida, Eric bumped into George Terry, a local guitarist whom Clapton had first met while recording *Layla*. The two started jamming together when Yvonne Elliman, who had appeared as Mary Magdalene in *Jesus Christ Superstar*, came by to sing and play guitar. Carl Radle showed up with drummer Jamie Oldaker and keyboardist Dick Sims from Tulsa, with the intention of forming a Dominos-like unit. Eric led the crew through some loose sessions, feeling out the musicians.

The studio was booked around the clock, 24 hours a day, so that the band could record whenever inspiration struck. They eventually laid down 30 tracks, and *461 Ocean Boulevard* was pieced together from weeks of casual jamming. The final product had much to do with Tom Dowd, who suggested spicing up the more subdued material with rowdier guitarwork. As Clapton told *Rolling Stone*, 'The groove we got into was so laid-back, so quiet and delicate, that I just thought, ''No, they won't want to hear it.'''

Eric, for his part, had come to Miami with only two numbers he was eager to do. One

Previous pages: Eric Clapton and his band in Sweden, June 1974, rehearsing for a lengthy tour.

Below left: In 1974, a rejuvenated Eric hit the road, playing to sports stadiums filled with 60,000-70,000 fans. In some cities, there were two sell-out shows a night.

Right: Clapton with Yvonne Elliman in Stockholm, June 1974. Elliman, born in Hawaii, portrayed Mary Magdalene in the stage and screen versions of *Jesus Christ Superstar.*

was 'Please Be With Me,' a 1971 track by the group Cowboy that Duane Allman had played on; Eric's smooth dobro lines and warm vocal make his version a fitting tribute to Duane. The other song was 'Give Me Strength,' a spiritual plea that he salvaged from that box of cassettes he had recorded during his three-year retreat. (Unfortunately, 'Give Me Strength' was deleted from later pressings of *461* because of copyright problems, but restored on the CD version of the album.)

Released in the summer of 1974, *461 Ocean Boulevard* was a strong comeback effort. All the ideas Clapton had been toying with during his hibernation cascaded forth, and the album in many ways picked up where *Eric Clapton* had left off. On songs like 'Steady Rollin' Man,' his vocals were robust, and the band could probe blues, reggae, and easy-going pop with equal skill. There were some old favorites from Eric's early days: Johnny Otis's R & B chestnut 'Willie and the Hand Jive,' plus blues standards by Elmore James and Robert Johnson. 'Let It Grow' had

Left: Clapton fans were often in for a treat during Eric's early-1970s concerts: he would start each show with two or three acoustic numbers.

shimmering washes of sound, along with sublime dobro playing. And while the LP elicited the usual cries for hotter guitar, the music glowed with communal warmth. 'I Shot the Sheriff,' a surprise number-one pop hit, hinted at Eric's growing infatuation with reggae. He loved the original version on Bob Marley's *Burnin'*, and at first, he didn't want his version on *461 Ocean Boulevard*, thinking it didn't measure up to the original.

The three-month American stadium tour for *461 Ocean Boulevard* was an ill-planned venture and almost sabotaged Clapton's return to the rock scene. Recording the album was one thing, but he was not psychologically strong enough to take the pressure of a tour. 'When I came off drugs,' he told Ray Coleman, 'I was left with a huge vacuum, a huge hole. . . . The only way I could fill it was with booze. . . . I was so drunk on some stages that I played lying on the stage flat on my back or staggering around wearing the weirdest combinations of clothes because I couldn't get it together even to dress pro-

perly.' Intent on letting his band share the spotlight, Eric would strum along, leaving most of the solo work to George Terry.

Like many of Clapton's subsequent tours, the 1974 outing did have some high points in the form of surprise walk-ons. Freddie King jammed with Eric at concerts in Buffalo and Jersey City; Pete Townshend, Keith Moon, and Joe Walsh showed up at various times. Before heading off to Japan and Europe, the band – which now included singer Marcy Levy, formerly with Bob Seger – recorded with Freddie King and flew to Jamaica to lay down tracks for *There's One in Every Crowd*.

'Japan was amazing,' Yvonne Elliman recalled to Barbara Charone in *Sounds*. 'They'd sit quietly through each song and at the end of every song they'd shout ''Rayra, Rayra, Rayra, Elic Crapton, Elic Crapton, Rayra'' . . . and as soon as we'd start ''Layla,'' they'd charge the stage. Boys would run up to kiss Eric . . . something about that song is magic. It frightens Eric when he sees how people act when they hear it.'

Opposite: Clapton as the Preacher in the film version of the rock opera *Tommy*, ably supported by the Who's John Entwistle and Pete Townshend.

Above: Eric and his band kicked off their 1974 U.S. tour at the Yale Bowl in New Haven, Connecticut, on 28 July. Clapton's onstage attire could be quite bizarre at that time.

The album *There's One in Every Crowd*, which appeared in April 1975, was critically blasted and sold poorly. The relaxed (some would say overly relaxed) mood was inspired, no doubt, by the lazy island setting; the vocals were hushed, the songs short on passion. It was also hard to tell which guitar tracks were Eric's and which were George Terry's. Though bound to disappoint Clapton fans the first time around, *There's One in Every Crowd* does improve with repeated listening, and it holds together even better than *461*. ('Better Make It Through Today,' matching Eric's grizzled vocal with an eloquent solo, was rescued from cut-out oblivion and added to later pressings of *461*.) As George Terry explained

Opposite: Yvonne Elliman and Eric. Elliman's full-bodied vocals added punch to the Clapton band's sound, as the *E.C. Was Here* album makes clear.

Overleaf: Here's an unusual venue: London's Crystal Palace Bowl, where fans 'soak up' the sounds of Clapton and company, 31 July 1976.

Above: 'In the blues format, I can almost lose consciousness,' Eric told *Guitar Player* in 1976. 'It's like seeing in the dark.'

to Barbara Charone, *461* 'had a few scattered parts, shades of different directions. *There's One in Every Crowd* kept it narrowed down to one certain thing – a sound.'

The long 1975 tour was a rousing success and a far cry from the booze-inspired excesses of the year before. The band (and George Terry in particular) prodded Eric more, and he rose to the challenge, especially on roof-raisers like 'Further On Up the Road.' He even played 'Sunshine of Your Love' for the first time since his days with Cream. Flashes of blues power burst forth on occasion, and it soon became clear that Clapton in concert was a much livelier musician than Clapton the studio artist. Carlos Santana, John McLaughlin, Joe Cocker, and Poco jammed with him on this tour, while Eric dropped by a Rolling Stones concert in New York to tear into 'Sympathy for the Devil' and guested on a Bob Dylan session.

There's One in Every Crowd had flopped commercially. Eric's record label, RSO, was in a hurry to cash in on the buzz being generated by his concerts, so Tom Dowd built a live album around 'Have You Ever Loved a Woman' to show that Eric could still sizzle on blues numbers. For the most part, *E.C. Was Here* did the trick. 'Driftin' Blues' and 'Can't Find My Way Home' treated fans to Clapton playing acoustic leads, and the electric work was exciting. 'Ramblin' on My Mind' rumbled at a slow burn, with Eric singing like a Delta bluesman – a far cry from the tentative and naive 1966 Bluesbreakers version. But for some strange reason, even though *E.C. Was Here* proved that Clapton the guitar hero was alive and kicking, the LP sold poorly.

Eric regained his commercial stride with *No Reason to Cry*, which he recorded in early 1976 at the Band's Shangri-La Studios. A stellar array of talent such as Dylan (singing with Clapton on 'Sign Language'), the Band, Ron Wood, George Harrison, and Billy Preston helped out. Eric clearly enjoyed the camaraderie, immersing himself in a country/pop sound and crafting bouncy tunes like 'Hello Old Friend' and 'Carnival.' But his guitar playing was mostly buried in the background, and the album's stand-out solo, on 'Sign Language,' was played by Robbie Robertson. The album was patchy and the musicianship lukewarm, although one highlight is Clapton's sputtering work-out on Otis Rush's 'Double Trouble.'

Eric later claimed that *No Reason to Cry* failed to capture the more inspired moments at Shangri-La. 'We cut something like 25 tracks in three weeks out of nowhere, out of the blue, it was just like falling rain,' he recalled in the notes to a 1979 tour program, 'and the outtakes – whoever's got them is sitting on a mint, because they're beautiful. Some of the best stuff didn't get on the album, like instrumentals.'

By the time *No Reason to Cry* came out, Eric was on a short British tour, which was livened up by jams with Larry Coryell, Freddie King, Ron Wood, and Van Morrison. At one

London concert, he accompanied country star Don Williams with some delicate dobro support. Later, he played with The Band at their farewell concert in San Francisco; *The Last Waltz* film and album featured a blazing version of 'Further On Up the Road' that had him trading riffs with Robbie Robertson. In case his fans had forgotten, the man could still play.

Clapton and company recorded *Slowhand* in 1977, during a hectic tour of England, Europe, and Japan. In a sense, *Slowhand* closed one chapter of Eric's solo career. This was his most consistent set to date, with songwriting and playing strongly influenced by J.J. Cale and Don Williams. Producer Glyn Johns' insistence on hard work in the studio – no half-baked jams allowed here – rubbed Eric the wrong way. But Johns drew top-notch musicianship from the band, and he coaxed the most aggressive guitarwork from Clapton since *Layla*. 'Lay Down Sally,' 'Wonderful Tonight,' and J.J. Cale's 'Cocaine' became concert staples; *Slowhand* reached number two on the album charts and generated a Top Ten single in 'Lay Down Sally'/ 'Cocaine.' After the album was finished, Yvonne Elliman left the band for a solo career.

Though Eric was not happy with his vocals, his playing on *Slowhand* was undeniably solid. There was subtle country picking, along with multilayered lead lines and guitar heroics. ('The Core' sported a time-stopping riff reminiscent of a moment during Clapton's solo on 'Yer Blues' [*Live Peace at Toronto*]). The album was a bookend of sorts, in that Eric wrote 'Wonderful Tonight,' a deceptively simple love song, for Patti Harrison – the same woman who inspired 'Layla,' and the woman he eventually married in 1979.

Above: Eric goes country & western. In 1976, he began immersing himself in the quiet sounds of country star Don Williams.

Opposite top: Phase 1 of Clapton's solo career. When released on CD in the 1980s, many of these albums featured bonus tracks.

Opposite bottom: Eric at last wedded his elusive Layla, marrying Patti Boyd Harrison on 27 March 1979 in Tucson, Arizona.

ERIC CLAPTON
461 OCEAN BOULE
E.C. WAS HERE
ERIC CLAPTON
SLOWHAND
ERIC CLAPTON
no reason to cry
Eric Clapton
There's one in every crowd

I've Got a Rock and Roll Heart – The Solo Years, Part Two

From *Slowhand* through the early 1980s, Clapton groped for a musical identity, meandering through a series of uneven recordings. Although sparks could still fly at his concerts – especially when Eric saluted the blues, as on a 1979 tour with Muddy Waters – albums like *Backless* and *Another Ticket* were lackluster affairs. He intentionally downplayed his guitar playing, taking a 'less-is-more' approach, but was roundly rebuked for it. His albums sold well, but this was not a creative or fulfilling period for Clapton.

In 1978, George Terry departed for a solo career, so Eric toured Europe with Carl Radle, Dick Sims, and Jamie Oldaker. The next year was an eventful one. He married Patti, toured with Muddy Waters, and retooled his band by bringing in Englishmen like guitarist Albert Lee, keyboardist Chris Stainton, bassist Dave Markee, and drummer Henry Spinetti. The live *Just One Night*, recorded at Tokyo's Budokan Theater, had some fine moments, with Albert Lee's country-flavored licks meshing nicely with Clapton's playing. Markee and Spinetti had backed Joan Armatrading on a few albums, but in this setting, they were unchallenging. And especially on the longer numbers, they were just too stiff to let Eric stretch out. *Another Ticket* – the only album that Clapton made with this band – was competent, and 'I Can't Stand It,' pulled as a single from the album, became a size-

Previous pages: Chuck Berry, Keith Richards, and Clapton playing together at a 60th Birthday Concert for Berry (filmed for *Hail! Hail Rock & Roll*) In October 1986.

Below: Eric during the 1975 U.S. tour. In Providence, Rhode Island, Clapton played 'Sunshine of Your Love' – the first time he had performed the song since Cream's breakup.

Above: The bespectacled blues master, 1979.

able hit. Apart from the authentically bluesy 'Floating Bridge,' though, *Another Ticket* was uninspired.

Eric's drinking problem had grown worse during the 1970s, and finally caught up with him in March 1981. Two weeks into an American tour, he collapsed onstage and was rushed to the hospital with ulcers, one of which was the size of an orange. After recovering, he appeared at an Amnesty International benefit known as the Secret Policeman's Other Ball in London that fall, jamming with Jeff Beck. He followed this up with a brief tour the next year. Otherwise, Clapton kept a low profile while he recuperated. Hints that he might be back on track came in the fall of 1982, during the recording of *Money & Cigarettes* in Nassau, the Bahamas. The British band was just not working out, so Eric fired them all (except for Albert Lee) and recruited Donald 'Duck' Dunn and drummer Roger Hawkins, two Muscle Shoals pros.

Money & Cigarettes, the cover of which sported a newly-sober Clapton elegantly attired in a suit, signaled a fresh musical approach – taut, funky, and spirited. Eric's vocals were stronger than ever; the songs, though still lightweight, were punchy; and the rhythm tracks had muscle. From the crisp drumming on 'Ain't Going Down' to Clapton's stinging licks over the rhumba beat of Albert King's 'Crosscut Saw,' *Money & Cigarettes* was a drastic improvement on the unfocused feel of Clapton's post-*Slowhand* output. This band pushed him hard on tour, too, and Eric responded with unusual verve.

In late 1983, Eric participated in a series of benefit concerts for Ronnie Lane and the Action Research into Multiple Sclerosis Fund in London. Steve Winwood, Jeff Beck, and Jimmy Page did separate sets, with a backing band that included Kenny Jones, Charlie Watts, and Bill Wyman. Guitar buffs went wild at the sight of Clapton, Beck, and Page – the

holy triumvirate of British rock guitar, and all former Yardbirds – lined up onstage, playing 'Tulsa Time,' 'Wee Wee Baby,' and 'Layla.' The next year, Eric guested as lead guitarist for Roger Waters' 'Pros and Cons of Hitch-hiking' tour, hoping to play sideman à la Delaney & Bonnie. It was an unwise move; he performed well, especially on the Pink Floyd numbers, but chainsmoked and generally looked bored onstage.

Clapton's turnaround came in 1985, when he picked up a new audience and regained his momentum. The assault came on two fronts: on record, with *Behind the Sun*'s 'Same Old Blues,' and in concert, with his much-lauded appearance at Live Aid.

Left: Jimmy Page, Clapton, Bill Wyman, and Jeff Beck at the ARMS concert in London, 20 September 1983.

Below: Eric at the ARMS concert in Los Angeles, 5 December 1983. Clapton, Jeff Beck, and Jimmy Page – ex-Yardbirds all – played together on 'Layla.'

Behind the Sun, produced by Phil Collins and released in March 1985, had a high-tech pop sheen. The album was blatantly commercial; in fact, when Eric submitted the tapes to Warner Bros., the corporate brass asked him to delete three tracks and record three new ones, including 'Forever Man.' (Two of those dropped songs, 'Heaven Is One Step Away' and 'Too Bad,' appear on the *Crossroads* compilation.) He wrote most of the songs using a synthesizer and a drum machine.

Despite the processed sound and a throw-away version of 'Knock On Wood,' *Behind the Sun* at least showcased Eric the guitarist – on J.J. Cale's 'Same Old Blues' and 'Just

Like A Prisoner,' he slices through the mix with some truly frantic playing. The story goes that during the sessions for the album, Clapton learned that everyone was trying to shield him from the heavy-duty partying going on among the bandmembers and crew. Furious at being treated like a child, Eric channeled his anger into 'Same Old Blues,' lashing out with his Fender and singing with such emotion that the original 'guide' vocal was never redone.

As if that recorded moment was not enough to show that Clapton hadn't lost it, there was the American tour to promote *Behind the Sun*. Tim Renwick replaced Albert Lee on second guitar; back-up singers Shaun Murphy and Marcy Levy added some vocal firepower behind Eric, who was in peak form. Suddenly, Clapton was all over the place. He made a video for 'Forever Man'; appeared with the house band on 'The David Letterman Show,' playing 'White Room'; jammed for three sets with Buddy Guy in Chicago; frequented one charity benefit after another; and shared the stage with artists like Phil Collins, Lionel Richie, Sting, Dire Straits, Carlos Santana, and Carl Perkins.

This was only the beginning of a burst of activity for Eric. His energetic set at the Live Aid concert in July 1985 – which included 'White Room,' 'She's Waiting,' and 'Layla' – reached millions of television viewers worldwide. At a show packed with sloppy performances, he proved that he was no 1960s relic, but rather a seasoned pro who could still deliver the goods. Clapton ventured into composing for film (*Homeboy, Lethal Weapon*) and TV ('Edge of Darkness,' a British TV miniseries), reaching a younger crowd with videos and knock-out live shows. He also did a number of interviews for publications like *Guitar Player, Rolling Stone,* and *Musician*. With the album *August*, he assembled a crack four-piece band with Phil Collins and drew rave reviews with a short club tour in 1986.

Over the past few years, Eric has been so busy that it's hard to keep up with him. The number of his surprise live appearances – with the Rolling Stones, Elton John, Jack Bruce, Little Feat, and Dire Straits, to name a few – is staggering. With this high visibility has come hefty commercial success. *Crossroads*, a 1988 boxed-set compilation spanning his 25 years in music, has gone platinum, as has his most recent album, *Journeyman*. And both *Crossroads* and *The Layla Ses-*

Page 82: Eric was in fine form for his set at the Live Aid show on 13 July 1985. Even long-time fans were surprised to hear 'White Room.'

Page 83: Clapton at the Prince's Trust Concert in London, 5 June 1987. George Harrison and Eric traded licks on 'While My Guitar Gently Weeps' – as they had at the Concert for Bangladesh in 1971.

Above: While Clapton's latter-day LPs have attracted mixed critical notices, their chart success is undeniable: six gold and two platinum albums.

Below: Mark Knopfler of Dire Straits played in Clapton's band in 1987 and 1988. Eric had jammed with Dire Straits years earlier.

Bottom left: In October 1985, Clapton joined George Harrison and other stars to film a TV tribute to Carl Perkins, 'Blue Suede Shoes.'

Bottom right: Phil Collins drummed behind Eric on several tours, producing tracks on *Behind the Sun* and *August*.

Right: George Harrison, Eric, Roseanne Cash, and Ringo Starr at London's Limehouse Studios, 21 October 1985. The occasion was the taping of a TV special on Carl Perkins.

Right: Clapton at a charity cricket match in England, 1990.

Below: Tragedy struck on 20 March 1991, when Eric's four-year-old son, Conor, fell to his death from an apartment building in which he lived with his mother, Italian actress Lori Del Santo.

These pages: How does Clapton approach taking a solo? He explained to *Guitar Player* in 1985: 'I really want to hit everybody, but it's got a lot to do with timing and space. The objective . . . is to make everyone feel like they've just been struck by a bolt of lightning. . . . Make them all wait for the first note of the solo, then hit exactly the right note so they're all satisfied.'

Below: 'I think I'm beginning to relax more at what I do,' Eric told *Guitar Player* in 1988. 'I don't feel I have to prove anything, and I really still do enjoy the work.'

Opposite: The guitar hero today, carrying on after 25 years in the music business.

sions, in unearthing rare and unissued recordings, have reaffirmed Clapton's legacy with older fans. In 1990, Eric performed an ambitious string of concerts at London's Royal Albert Hall: six nights with a four-piece band, six nights with a thirteen-piece group, three Blues Nights with Robert Cray and Buddy Guy, and three nights backed by the National Philarmonic Orchestra. (These shows were recorded for a video release and a double album.) He was also a guest on 'Saturday Night Live,' and played at Knebworth.

Having pulled through a decade-long slump, Eric Clapton is back on top. He seems to have reached a compromise between recording commercial material and championing traditional blues classics onstage and on record, such as Bobby 'Blue' Bland's 'Further On Up the Road,' Ray Charles' 'Hard Times,' and Albert King's 'Crosscut Saw.' His loyal fans still cry out for 'Layla,' but no one expects him to turn in marathon performances like the thirteen-minute version of 'Steppin' Out' on *Live Cream Volume 2*. The shy, insecure bandleader of the 1970s is now the self-assured journeyman of the 1990s – as obsessive about his music as he was when he first heard the blues.

Discography

SINGLES

This listing does not include promotional singles or 12″ versions where 12″ is an alternate version of a 45.

	Release Date
The Yardbirds:	
I Wish You Would/A Certain Girl	Jul 1964
Good Morning Little Schoolgirl/I Ain't Got You	Oct 1964
For Your Love/Got to Hurry	Feb 1965
John Mayall's Bluesbreakers:	
I'm Your Witch Doctor/Telephone Blues	Oct 1965
Lonely Years/Bernard Jenkins	Aug 1966
Key To Love/Parchman Farm	Sep 1966
Cream:	
Wrapping Paper/Cat's Squirrel	Oct 1966
I Feel Free/N.S.U.	Dec 1966
Strange Brew/Tales of Brave Ulysses	Jun 1967
Spoonful/Spoonful, Part 2 [US only]	1967
Sunshine of Your Love/SWLABR*	Dec 1967
Anyone For Tennis/Pressed Rat and Warthog	May 1968
White Room/Those Were the Days**	Oct 1968
Crossroads/Passing the Time [US only]	Jan 1969
Badge/What a Bringdown	Apr 1969
Sweet Wine [live]/Lawdy Mama [US only]	1970
Delaney & Bonnie:	
Comin' Home/Superstar	Dec 1969
Eric Clapton:	
After Midnight/Easy Now	Oct 1970
Derek & the Dominos:	
Tell the Truth/Roll It Over	Aug 1970 [withdrawn]
Bell Bottom Blues/Keep On Growing	Feb 1971
Layla/I Am Yours	Mar 1971
Layla/Bell Bottom Blues [re.]	May 1972
Why Does Love Got to Be So Sad/Presence of the Lord [live]	Apr 1973

Eric Clapton:

Let It Rain/Easy Now [US only]***	Sep 1972
Bell Bottom Blues/Little Wing [US only]****	Feb 1973
I Shot the Sheriff/Give Me Strength	Jul 1974
Willie and the Hand Jive/Mainline Florida	Oct 1974
Swing Low Sweet Chariot/Pretty Blue Eyes	Apr 1975
Knocking On Heaven's Door/Someone Like You	Aug 1975
Hello Old Friend/All Our Past Times	Oct 1976
Carnival/Hungry	Feb 1977
Lay Down Sally/Next Time You See Her	Nov 1977
Wonderful Tonight/Peaches and Diesel	Mar 1978
Cocaine/Tulsa Time	1978
Promises/Watch Out for Lucy	Sep 1978
If I Don't Be There by Morning/Tulsa Time	Feb 1979
Tulsa Time/Cocaine [live] [US only]	Jun 1980
Blues Power/Early in the Morning [live] [US only]	Oct 1980
I Can't Stand It/Black Rose	Feb 1981
Another Ticket/Rita Mae	Apr 1981
Layla [re.]/Wonderful Tonight [live]	Feb 1982
I Shot the Sheriff/Cocaine [re.]	May 1982
I've Got a Rock and Roll Heart/Man In Love	Jan 1983
The Shape You're In/Crosscut Saw	Mar 1983
Slow Down Linda/Crazy Country Hop	May 1983
Forever Man/Too Bad	Feb 1985
See What Love Can Do	Mar 1985
She's Waiting/Jailbait	Jun 1985
It's In the Way That You Use It/The Grand Illusion	Mar 1987
Tearing Us Apart (with Tina Turner)	Jun 1987
Pretending	Nov 1989
Bad Love	Mar 1990

*Released Sept. 1968 in the U.K.
**Released Jan. 1969 in the U.K.
***Reissue from *Eric Clapton At His Best* compilation
****Reissue from *Clapton* compilation; credited to 'Eric Clapton'

ALBUMS

	Release Date
The Yardbirds:	
Five Live Yardbirds	Jan 1965
Sonny Boy Williamson and the Yardbirds	Jan 1966
John Mayall's Bluesbreakers:	
Bluesbreakers with Eric Clapton	Jul 1966
Primal Solos [rec. 1966]	Jan 1977
Cream:	
Fresh Cream*	Dec 1966
Disraeli Gears	Nov 1967
Wheels of Fire**	Aug 1968
Goodbye***	Mar 1969
Live Cream	Jun 1970
Live Cream, Volume 2	Jul 1972
Blind Faith:	
Blind Faith	Aug 1969
Delaney and Bonnie:	
On Tour	Jun 1970
Eric Clapton:	
Eric Clapton	Aug 1970
Derek & the Dominos:	
Layla and Other Assorted Love Songs	Dec 1970
The Layla Sessions [rec. 1970]	Nov 1990
In Concert	Mar 1973
Eric Clapton:	
Eric Clapton's Rainbow Concert	Sep 1973
461 Ocean Boulevard	Aug 1974
There's One in Every Crowd	Apr 1975
E.C. Was Here****	Aug 1975

SELECTED GUEST APPEARANCES/SESSION WORK

Champion Jack Dupree, *From New Orleans to Chicago* (1966)
Aretha Franklin, *Lady Soul* (1968)
The Beatles, *The White Album* (1968)
Billy Preston, *That's the Way God Planned It* (1969)
John Lennon/Plastic Ono Band, *Live Peace in Toronto 1969* (1969)
Leon Russell, *Leon Russell* (1970)
Doris Troy, *Doris Troy* (1970)
George Harrison, *All Things Must Pass* (1970)
Stephen Stills, *Stephen Stills* (1970)
John Mayall, *Back to the Roots* (1971)
Buddy Guy & Junior Wells, *Play the Blues* (1971)
Howlin' Wolf, *The London Howlin' Wolf Sessions* (1971)

No Reason to Cry*****	Aug 1976
Slowhand	Nov 1977
Backless******	Nov 1978
Just One Night	May 1980
Another Ticket	Feb 1981
Money and Cigarettes	Feb 1983
Behind the Sun	Mar 1985
August	Feb 1987
Journeyman	Nov 1989
24 Nights	Oct 1991

Compilations:
The Blues World of Eric Clapton (1975)
Best of Cream (1969)
Heavy Cream (1972)
[Cream] Off the Top (1973)
Strange Brew: The Very Best of Cream (1983)
History of Eric Clapton (1972)
Eric Clapton at His Best (1972)
Clapton (1973)
Time Pieces – The Best of Eric Clapton (1982)
Time Pieces, Volume 2 – Live in the Seventies (1983)
Backtrackin' (1984)
The Cream of Eric Clapton (1987)
Crossroads (1988)

*Early versions of *Fresh Cream* had 'I Feel Free' but not 'Spoonful.' *Cream*, a 1975 British reissue, added 'Wrapping Paper' and 'The Coffee Song,' an obscure B-side. The CD version of *Fresh Cream* now includes all these tracks.

**This double album was also released as two separate albums – the studio LP and the live LP – in England.
***CD version adds the single 'Anyone for Tennis.'
****CD version has full-length version of 'Ramblin' on My Mind.'
*****CD version adds bonus track, 'Last Night.'
******CD version has extended version of 'Early In the Morning.'

Dr. John, *The Sun, Moon and Herbs* (1971)
George Harrison, *Concert for Bangladesh* (1972)
John Lennon/Plastic Ono Band, *Sometime in New York City* (1972)
Tommy [Soundtrack] (1975)
Bob Dylan, *Desire* (1976)
Stephen Bishop, *Careless* (1976)
Freddie King, *1934-1976* (1977)
Ronnie Lane/Pete Townshend, *Rough Mix* (1977)
The Band, *The Last Waltz* (1978)
Phil Collins, *Face Value* (1981)
Various Artists, *The Secret Policeman's Other Ball* (1982)
Roger Waters, *The Pros and Cons of Hitch-hiking* (1984)
Jack Bruce, *Willpower* (1987)

Index

Page numbers in *italics* indicate illustrations